verbs

by Viv Lambert
illustrated by Andrew Everitt-Stewart

In the morning.

Wake up.

Get up.

Brush my
teeth.

Comb my
hair.

Smile in the mirror.

Wash my
face.

Get dressed.

Drink juice.

Eat breakfast.

At home.

Make a cake.

Turn on the computer.

Have my lunch.

Sweep the floor.

Watch TV.

Tidy my room.

Cook some food.

Clean the windows.

At school.

Spell my name.   Take an apple.

Write a story.   Paint a picture.

Count the pencils.

Clap my hands.

Cut out my picture.

Draw a square.

Colour the animals.

With my friends.

Sing a song.

Talk to friends.

Pretend to be
a princess.

Hide behind
a tree.

Hold hands. Share a snack.

Whisper a
secret.

Laugh at
a joke.

At the weekend.

Listen to music.

Dance at the party.

Look at the animals.

Play the piano.

Wear my trainers.

Play football.

Skate in the park.

Give a present.

Swim in the pool.

In the park.

Ride a bike.

Fly a kite.

Run round
the track.

Skip with a rope.

Sail a boat.   See my friends.

Kick a ball.   Walk the dog.

In the garden.

Throw a ball.

Catch a ball.

Pick a flower.

Climb a tree.

Plant some
seeds.

Dig a hole.

Jump in the
sand.

Water the
flowers.

Children...

Fall over.

Cry for Mummy.

Learn a game.

Lose the ball.

Find a shell.

Fight over toys.

Stand up.

Sit down.

Grown ups...

Phone someone.   Work hard.

Look after me.

Shout
sometimes.

Love me.

Go out.

Give me presents.

Help me.

In town.

Wait for
the bus.

Stop the bus.

Get on the bus.

Get off the bus.

Meet a friend.   Drive a car.

Build a road.   Shop for clothes.

Going shopping.

Smell fresh bread.

Taste some cheese.

Choose a cake.

Carry a bag.

Buy magazines.

Push a
trolley. Pay the shopkeeper.

Weigh some fruit. Buy a comic.

Bedtime.

Have a bath.

Go to bed.

Read a story.

Switch off the light

Hug my teddy.

Kiss Daddy.

Sleep all night.

Dream sweet
dreams.

First Skills

Ideal for children aged 2 years and upwards, the **First Skills** readers, activity books and flash cards are designed for parents to help young children develop basic skills in early maths, language and writing.

Readers

Flash cards

Sticker activity books

Other books in this series

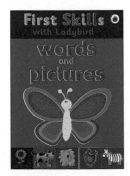